PIANO • VOCAL • GUITAR

R&B HITS of the '60s

ISBN 0-7935-7183-9

HAL•LEONARD®
CORPORATION
7777 W. BLUEMOUND RD. P.O. BOX 13819 MILWAUKEE, WI 53213

Visit Hal Leonard Online at
www.halleonard.com

R & B HITS OF THE '60s

Contents

AIN'T NOTHING LIKE THE REAL THING

Words and Music by NICKOLAS ASHFORD
and VALERIE SIMPSON

AIN'T TOO PROUD TO BEG

Words and Music by EDWARD HOLLAND
and NORMAN WHITFIELD

2. Now I've heard a cryin' man
Is half a man with no sense of pride,
But if I have to cry to keep you,
I don't mind weepin' if it'll keep you by my side.
(Chorus)

3. If I have to sleep on your doorstep all night and day
Just to keep you from walking away,
Let your friends laugh, even this I can stand,
'Cause I wanna keep you any way I can.
(Chorus)

4. Now I've got a love so deep in the pit of my heart,
And each day it grows more and more,
I'm not ashamed to call and plead to you, baby,
If pleading keeps you from walking out that door.
(Chorus)

BABY I NEED YOUR LOVIN'

Words and Music by BRIAN HOLLAND,
LAMONT DOZIER and EDWARD HOLLAND

beg. _____   Then weak I'd ___ rath-er be, ___   If   it means hav-

ing   you   to   keep, ___   "Cause late - ly   I've   been los-ing sleep. ___

Chorus:

Ba -   by, I need ___ your lov - in';   Got ___ to have all ___ your lov - in'.

Ba -   by I need ___ your lov - in';   Got ___ to have all ___ your lov - in'.

Lonely nights echo your name, Oh, some-times I won-der will I ev-er be the same? Oh yeah!

When you see me smil-ing, you know things have got-ten worse.

An-y smile you might see has all been re-hearsed.

BERNADETTE

Words and Music by BRIAN HOLLAND,
LAMONT DOZIER and EDWARD HOLLAND

BABY LOVE

Words and Music by BRIAN HOLLAND,
EDWARD HOLLAND and LAMONT DOZIER

COME SEE ABOUT ME

Words and Music by LAMONT DOZIER,
BRIAN HOLLAND and EDWARD HOLLAND

DANCING IN THE STREET

Words and Music by MARVIN GAYE,
IVY HUNTER and WILLIAM STEVENSON

Call - ing out ___ a - round __ the world, "Are you
in - vi - ta - tion a - cross the na - tion, a

it does-n't mat-ter _____ what you wear __ just as

long as you are__ there.__ So come on, _ ev - 'ry guy_

grab a girl. __ Ev - 'ry - where ___ a - round_

___ the world___ they'll be ___ danc - ing. ___

DO YOU LOVE ME

Words and Music by
BERRY GORDY

GET READY

Words and Music by
WILLIAM "SMOKEY" ROBINSON

GOING TO A GO-GO

Words and Music by WILLIAM "SMOKEY" ROBINSON, MARVIN TARPLIN,
WARREN MOORE and ROBERT ROGERS

Chorus

HEATWAVE
(Love Is Like a Heatwave)

Words and Music by EDWARD HOLLAND,
LAMONT DOZIER and BRIAN HOLLAND

I CAN'T GET NEXT TO YOU

Words and Music by BARRETT STRONG
and NORMAN WHITFIELD

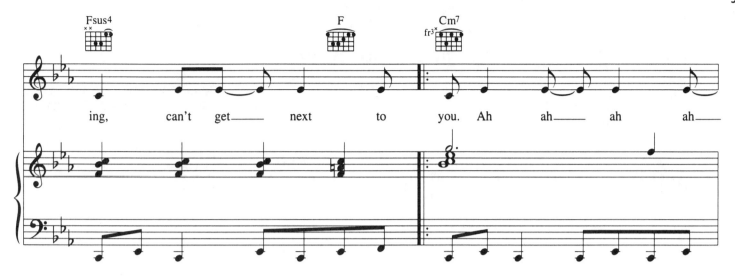

Verse 2:
I can fly like a bird in the sky
And I can buy anything that money can buy.
I can turn a river into a raging fire
I can live forever if I so desire.
I don't want it, all these things I can do
'Cause I can't get next to you.

Verse 3:
I can turn back the hands of time - you better believe I can
I can make the seasons change just by waving my hand.
I can change anything from old to new
The thing I want to do the most I'm unable to do.
I'm an unhappy woman with all the powers I possess
'Cause man, you're the key to my happiness.

I CAN'T HELP MYSELF
(Sugar Pie, Honey Bunch)

Words and Music by BRIAN HOLLAND,
LAMONT DOZIER and EDWARD HOLLAND

Moderately fast

Su - gar - pie, hon - ey bunch, you know that I
Su - gar - pie, hon - ey bunch, I'm weak - er than a

love you. _
man should be. I can't help my - self,
I can't help my - self,

MY GIRL

Words and Music by WILLIAM "SMOKEY" ROBINSON
and RONALD WHITE

I've got sun- shine____

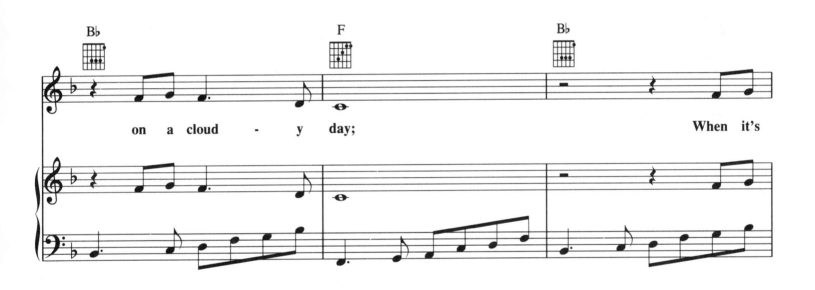

on a cloud - y day;   When it's

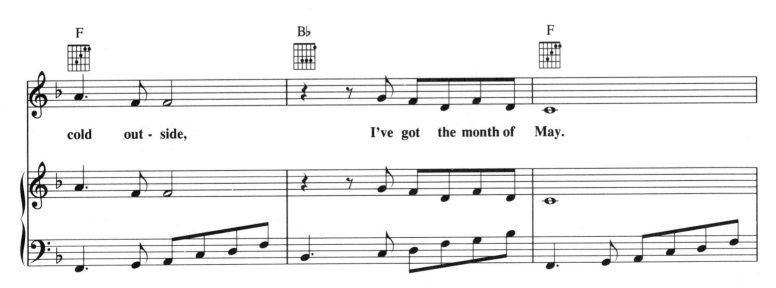

cold out - side,   I've got the month of May.

I HEARD IT THROUGH THE GRAPEVINE

Words and Music by NORMAN J. WHITFIELD
and BARRETT STRONG

I SECOND THAT EMOTION

Words and Music by WILLIAM "SMOKEY" ROBINSON
and ALFRED CLEVELAND

NOWHERE TO RUN

Words and Music by LAMONT DOZIER,
BRIAN HOLLAND and EDDIE HOLLAND

OOO BABY BABY

Words and Music by WILLIAM "SMOKEY" ROBINSON
and WARREN MOORE

SHOTGUN

Words and Music by
AUTRY DeWALT

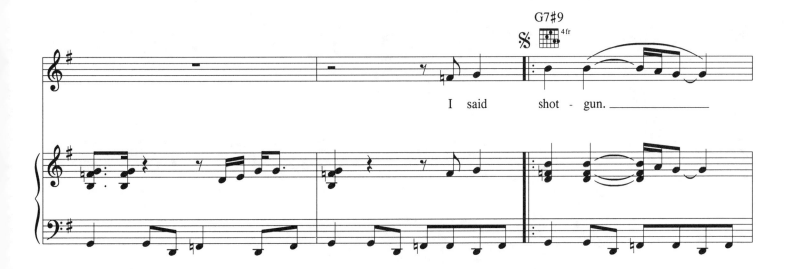

I said shot - gun.

Shoot him 'fore he run now.
Do the jerk, ba - by. ___

Do the jerk now. ___
I said it's

cry - in' time.
I said it's cry - in' time. Hey.

Repeat ad lib. and Fade

PLEASE MR. POSTMAN

Words and Music by ROBERT BATEMAN, GEORGIA DOBBINS, WILLIAM GARRETT,
FREDDIE GORMAN and BRIAN HOLLAND

1. There must be some word to-day from my boy-friend so
2. (See additional lyrics)
3. (Instrumental solo, ad lib)

far a-way. Please, Mis-ter Post-man, look and see.

Verse 2:
So many days have passed me by.
You saw the tears in my eyes.
You wouldn't stop to make me feel better
By leavin' me a card or a letter.

STANDING IN THE SHADOWS OF LOVE

Words and Music by EDWARD HOLLAND,
LAMONT DOZIER and BRIAN HOLLAND

STOP! IN THE NAME OF LOVE

Words and Music by LAMONT DOZIER,
BRIAN HOLLAND and EDWARD HOLLAND

THE TRACKS OF MY TEARS

Words and Music by WILLIAM "SMOKEY" ROBINSON,
WARREN MOORE and MARVIN TARPLIN

might be _____ laugh - in' loud _____ and heart - y,
may be _____ cute, she's just a sub - sti - tute be - cause

deep in - side ___ I'm blue. ___
you're the per - ma - nent one. ___
So take a good look at my

face. You'll see my smile ___ looks out of place.
Look a lit - tle bit

clos - er, it's eas - y to trace the tracks of ___ my _____ tears. ___
clos - er,

THE WAY YOU DO THE THINGS YOU DO

Words and Music by WILLIAM "SMOKEY" ROBINSON
and ROBERT ROGERS

YOU KEEP ME HANGIN' ON

Words and Music by EDWARD HOLLAND,
LAMONT DOZIER and BRIAN HOLLAND

way you've got-ten o-ver me. _____ You say __ al - though __

we __ broke up __ you still wan-na be just friends.

But how can we still __ be friends __ when see-ing you on - ly breaks my

heart a - gain? ___ *(Spoken:)* *And there ain't nothing I can do about it.*

YOU'VE REALLY GOT A HOLD ON ME

Words and Music by
WILLIAM "SMOKEY" ROBINSON

I don't_____ like you,_____ but I_____ love you;
I don't_____ want you,_____ but I_____ need you;
I wan-na leave you,_____ don't wan-na stay here;

Seems that I'm al-ways_____ think-ing of you._____
Don't wan-na kiss you,_____ but I_____ need to.
Don't wan-na spend_____ an-oth-er day here._____

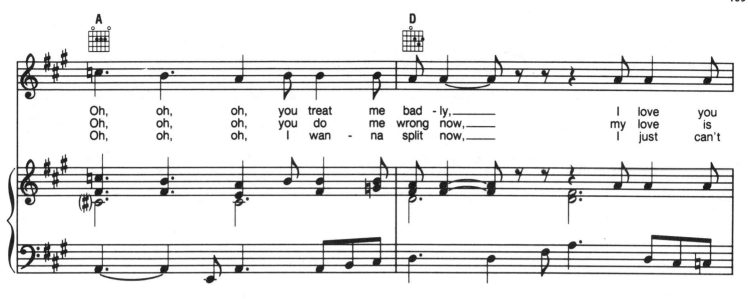

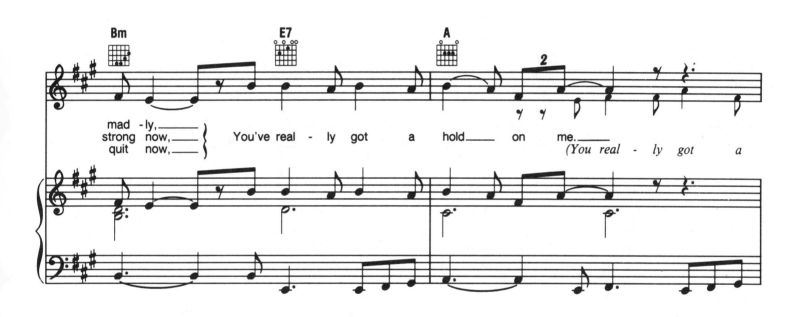

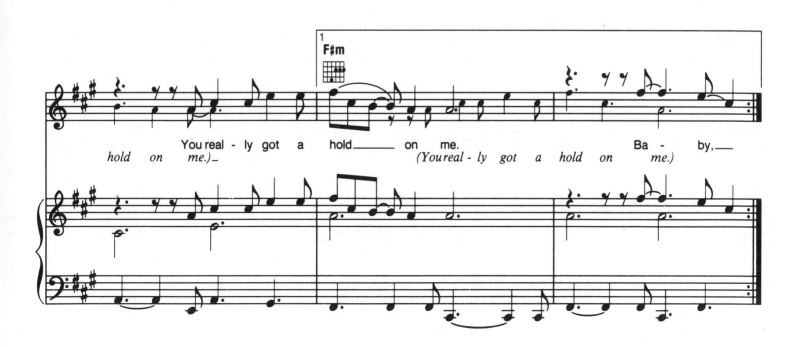

THE HISTORY OF ROCK

The most definitive set of rock songbooks ever published! Each book contains over 30 big hits arranged for piano, voice and guitar, as well as a detailed rock history of the times – complete with photos and chart records of the songs. Every rock historian and fan will want to make this series part of their collection.

BIRTH OF ROCK AND ROLL

The first volume explores rock's rhythm and blues roots and its earliest tunes – from "Rocket '88" and "Shake, Rattle And Roll" to the major hits of Elvis Presley, Little Richard, Jerry Lee Lewis, Buddy Holly, and more. 37 songs, including: All Shook Up • Blueberry Hill • Blue Suede Shoes • Earth Angel • Heartbreak Hotel • Long Tall Sally • Lucille • Goodnight, It's Time To Go • The Green Door • Rock Around The Clock • Tutti-Frutti • and more! 136 pages.
00490216...$12.95

THE LATE '50S

The declaration "Rock And Roll Is Here To Stay" led the way for American Bandstand greats like Paul Anka, Frankie Avalon, Fabian, Bobby Darin, and Connie Francis. This book also explores the novelty song hits, the close harmony styles, and romantic ballads that filled the radio waves. 48 songs, including: At The Hop • Chantilly Lace • Do You Want To Dance? • Great Balls Of Fire • Lollipop • Rock And Roll Is Here To Stay • Sea Of Love • Splish Splash • Tears On My Pillow • Tequila • Wake Up, Little Susie • Yakety Yak • and more. 176 pages.
00490321...$14.95

THE EARLY '60S

Surf music, doo wop, and dance crazes set the stage for a new decade. This volume explores the success of the Beach Boys, "Big Girls Don't Cry," and the Twist. 56 songs, including: Barbara Ann • Breaking Up Is Hard To Do • Do Wah Diddy Diddy • Duke Of Earl • Hit The Road, Jack • Louie, Louie • My Boyfriend's Back • Runaway • Sherry • Surfin' U.S.A. • Tell Laura I Love Her • The Twist • Under The Boardwalk • Wooly Bully • and more. 184 pages.
00490322...$15.95

THE MID '60S

The British invaded the charts and Hendrix re-invented the guitar in this volume, featuring chart toppers of the Beatles, the Moody Blues, the Hollies, Rolling Stones, Mamas and the Papas, James Brown, the Byrds, and many more. 49 songs, including: All Day And All Of The Night • California Dreamin' • Can't Buy Me Love • Dedicated To The One I Love • For Your Love • Gloria • Groovin' • Help! • Hey Joe • I Want To Hold Your Hand • Papa's Got A Brand New Bag • Summer In The City • Wild Thing • Yesterday • and more. 200 pages.
00490581...$15.95

THE LATE '60S

The turbulence of this era created a new mood for rock and roll. From the classic "Sgt. Pepper's Lonely Hearts Club Band" to the San Francisco sound and Janis Joplin to the jazz/rock hits of Blood, Sweat and Tears, you'll find the songs that made the statements of the time in this volume. 47 songs, including: Abraham, Martin And John • And When I Die • Born To Be Wild • Come Together • Hey Jude • Incense And Peppermints • The Letter • The Magic Bus • San Francisco (Be Sure To Wear Some Flowers In Your Hair) • Spinning Wheel • The Sunshine Of Your Love • White Room • A Whiter Shade Of Pale. 190 pages.
00311505...$15.95

THE EARLY '70S

The Beatles broke up, Southern bands brought their brand of rock and roll to the top of the charts, heavy metal was just in its infancy, and "American Pie" glorified the day the music died. Cooper and Bowie made rock a spectacle while the Moody Blues made it an art. From Black Sabbath to Neil Diamond, David Bowie to Elton John, the early 70's were a breeding ground for music superstars still around today. Features 45 hits, including: American Pie • Fire And Rain • Imagine • Maggie May • Rikki Don't Lose That Number • Sweet Home Alabama • and more. 208 pages.
00311538...$15.95

Prices, contents, and availability subject to change without notice.

FOR MORE INFORMATION, SEE YOUR LOCAL MUSIC DEALER, OR WRITE TO:

HAL•LEONARD® CORPORATION

7777 W. BLUEMOUND RD. P.O. BOX 13819 MILWAUKEE, WI 53213

THE LATE '70S

In the late '70s the piano men – Sedaka, John, and Joel – shared the charts with Kansas, Foreigner, and Aerosmith. Earth Wind and Fire, the Ohio Players, and the Sylvers kept funk and soul alive. Women fought for equality and won on the charts with Streisand, Tyler, Ronstadt and Gaynor on top. Underground grumblings of black leather punk began while the music of the Bee Gees and Donna Summer kept people in white satin dancing all night. 43 hits, including: Bad Case Of Loving You • Bennie And The Jets • Dust In The Wind • Hot Blooded • I Will Survive • Piano Man • Walk This Way • and more. 208 pages.
00311603...$15.95

THE EARLY '80S

The last dregs of disco were cleaned off the charts by new wave, punk, contemporary hit radio, and heavy metal. The rock heavyweights – John Lennon, Paul McCartney, Stevie Wonder, Chicago, Billy Joel – shared the charts with slick newcomers – Human League, Culture Club, Eurythmics, Police – and the women of rock – Tina Turner, Joan Jett, Cyndi Lauper, Pat Benatar, and many more. 42 songs, including: Do You Really Want To Hurt Me • Every Breath You Take • I Love Rock 'N' Roll • Maniac • Owner Of A Lonely Heart • Sweet Dreams (Are Made Of This) • Total Eclipse Of The Heart • What's Love Got To Do With It • Woman • and more.
00311619...$15.95

THE LATE '80S

Shut up and dance became the war cry of 80s rock as videos paved the way for glamorous new stars. There were New Kids On The Block, Paula Abdul, Bobby Brown, Milli Vanilli, and those who had been around the block: Sting, Foreigner, Beach Boys, James Brown, and Robert Palmer. Megastars Michael Jackson, Madonna, Bon Jovi, and U2 shot to the top of the charts as rap started easing its way up to the mainstream. 43 songs, including: Addicted To Love • Careless Whisper • Hangin' Tough • If You Love Somebody Set Them Free • Kokomo • Livin' On A Prayer • My Prerogative • Red, Red Wine • Straight Up • We Didn't Start The Fire • You Give Love A Bad Name • and more.
00311620...$16.95